# MARKED PAPER

GW00726918

# MARKED PAPER

David Lockwood

First Impression—December 1995

ISBN 1 85902 375 4

Printed in Wales by
Gomer Press, Llandysul, Dyfed

For
Kate Goodwin
of Bath, a lover
of music, poetry
and pictures.

# CONTENTS

# THE OLD PHOTOGRAPH

It is odd to hold happiness in your hand,
such brightly focussed joy.
The sun shines in this photo
with one corner turned.

I peer to prove the time and place,
the place I know so well,
the time evades exactitude;
white blouses with dark cloth skirts
were undress uniform
in this century's teens,
from the daughter of a Tsar to
the suddenly monied and so emancipated
munition girl.

I read the faces and I learn
release, relief, a spectre gone.
I hover on a clue.
Then I see an eager, happy girl,
slim hands around her knees
with buckled shoes pointing
without suspicion to a ready future.
It is my mother!
Undaunted and prettier than I ever knew.
By her the time is rung.
Age eighteen. Year nineteen-nineteen.

The colonel almost at ease is freed of fears for his sons.
Jack with a jaunty cigarette
can plan and live his subsequent career.
Fred, white flannelled with a paper
folded to the sporting page
cares more for cricket scores
than plans for peace in mirrored halls.
His neat head will rise,
thinning to importance in a woollen city bank.

One woman stands, envelope in hand.
She shares their full-blown felicity
but
it is tempered by blows of loss.
She is the sibyl among them
looking fore and back,
not quite one of them.
She and I merge,
I hope her burden is not as mine.
I know too much,
their future is my past.
It sharpens empathy.

But, but, trumpet the gladness of that day,
the soul in a camera's click.
They relied on a like morrow.
Rejoice with them in the sun.
It is a rarity to hold
such happiness in your hand.

## LLWYNDAFYDD OAKS

Limbs interlace
imposing patterns on the sky,
a symmetraphobic trellis.
No striplings, all grown men
vigorous, proud but bending
in their cwm, living with
the western wind.

Boys, men, girls too
around them
yearned eastwards
leaving land to fill
foundries, mines,
classrooms, pulpits too.
Some returned but briefly.

The oaks remained
rooted.
They nourished the land
that nurtured them:
a subtle symbiosis.

# RITUAL

Shining in the electric light,
a bare bulb in a meagre shop,
a plate of pomegranates;
Emblem of vulgarity
to be shunned.

Looking, I wavered in my desire.
He who wished my friendship,
entered and from a prim purse
paid.
Forbidden fruit in my hand.
He was an important catalyst,
a releasing Eve,
cutting taboos
kept by loyalty and love.

A grown child
wandering in an adult world
unquestioning.
The pomegranate broke the seal,
missed youth emerged:
the 'fair ground fruit'
was tasted, enjoyed,
like fish and chips.
Accepted social parameters shuddered
and I was more alive.

So each year a pomegranate,
burnished like a well-worn saddle,
red like life,
primed with pips,
pitted with experience
enters my room,
symbol of escape
and freedom gained.

## ONE SKULL

Janus with his two faces
chases me throughout the year.
"Because", says my cousin,
"you are a Gemini."
I disagree.

Today, on the Begwns, in a hollow,
I found a skull, a lamb,
six days, no more.
Crisp paper bones
linked with a still articulated spine;
rib cage with too much air;
small teeth complete.
There were concavities curved and contoured
where shallow convex eyes should be.
This is a structure
of evolved refinement
cantilevered and curtailed correctly,
yet doomed and dead.
It alerts my intelligence
into scientific appreciation.

Turning this small light head,
there is a surprise,
a furry face, an ear.
The same evolution clothed
in soft white wool.

Two faces, one sheep,
indivisible.
It is not good, it is not evil,
certainly it is youth not age,
Not even life and death.
It is a unity.
It is head and heart
in one.
It is ego, it is id
in one small skull.
It is intellect,
it is emotion.
Above all it is one.

I look up,
Janus grins and agrees.

# THE JEWEL OF MOSCOW

Rain clattered like spent bullets,
thunder rolled like Verdun guns.
Appropriate: our destination lay
before the first World War.

A broad young smile
transformed a sad Slav face
and obliterated our lost fears.
"Yes, Sadovaya Kodrinskaya
was but one street away."

It was a cubic Hell, a grey Hell,
high blocks to house the numbered
more than named.

The house where humanity dwelt,
dwells, was dwarfed.

The gate, the garden, not weed-free,
the penthouse roof,
the hall, the bust, the wreath
were right. Appropriate again,
no more.

Upstairs, in a case, set angled,
as if for his nose,
the pince-nez.

Oval discs of glass ground
precisely.
Springs coiled as if by busy ants
and ivory pressure pads
and a chain, fine as a spider's thread;
strong delicacy.
Jewellery with purpose,
necessary accoutrements
for a certain man.
These are the real jewels of Moscow.
not the Fabergé precious toys
for jaded kings.

An instrument enabling
a man, a certain man, to see.

An accessory of gold and glass
giving vision to Chekhov.
Allowing him to see
more than most and
to comment resoundingly
with words, often unspoken,
unwritten too.

The real jewel of Moscow.

# EXILE

"In warmth to linger out my life."
She looks to the garden where her man
ties his bold procreative tomato plants.
It is difficult to see
in that wizened simian,
the young Corsican
virile, vibrant and always daring
and with charm, when it suited him.
He withers, dries.
"He's like an old olive,
still productive."

She turned to the mirror,
very faded Regency,
tailored in well-cut dust.
It, too, was an English aristocrat
in exile.
The mirror would have mirrored her
even had there been no glass.

A sigh, a sweeping look
the sea. "So beautiful, so blue."
The curtain billowed
it ushered in the scent,
the pungency of the wild maquis.
She smiled, "He had been heady, too."

A sigh for she saw her shelves,
a shrine. Photos of three
English kings, all signed.
Christmas cards from more recent Queens.
A little curled, creased
but complete and up to date.

The monkey man strides up the path,
swings in the window, supple still.
He wipes a film of dust from the cup.
He cares.
She sighs, she trails.
He gets on with the job. He always did.

# AGAINST THE HORDES

Am I mad
to think so often of that room
within the Arctic Circle?
Where a long case clock ticks
new time with an old voice,
defying the wind and ever ice
which makes its own slow dance
of advance and shy retreat.

The room's possessor
writes, records
old tales of Lapps.
This is a continuance of man's measure:
a signal of a hopeful future.
It augurs well.
Marked paper is potent.

# MEMORIAL TABLET, ABEREDW 1709

The black bow on his wife's bodice
danced and undid him:
it rose and curtsied with every sigh.

Those large and longed for eyes,
which had struggled to express
so much unknown for eleven weeks,
fluttered finally and closed.

He prayed, he cursed
and thundered imprecations
down the gorge at God
and any who cared to overhear.

At home he picked up the coverlet,
anticipation in each embroidered stitch.
He had drawn, she had sewn
three birds, lions, two tulips,
roses, violets, berries
and an angel.

It was copied on the stone
with his, James Davies', verse.

The pale thin man in black,
the old mason's vigour
shone through the dust.
Youth so old
and age so young.

The lines gathered.
Done.

Tears ran.
"Oh God, I meant so much more."
"O Lord, it is hard the hour to pass."
"Price, Price, put that down."
Set on the southern wall
beneath the eaves,
the letters, lions, berries, birds
and blooms have long outlasted
parents and the counterpane.

Still his words cut,
"It is hard ye hour to pass."

NINE POEMS
from
PICTURES
by
KEITH ANDREW

## I  The Parlour

The room's silence marks
starkly the tickless clock
that stands tock still.

The boy at the table
turns a page,
a rustle,a sigh,
a shift of feet.

He looks up around
the clock, the papered wall
and over-enlarged sepia icons
of his grand dad and mum:
accepted but unseen.
He really sees the light
still falling through
the stiffened lace.
Beyond the window the world,
slate water tank, pump
and the kennelled dog
and beyond that, more.

Ambition flickered
growing flames,
a world to win,
This room to escape.
So Latin once more claimed his mind,
his eye, intent.
He bent again.

He won but was never
to escape that room.
It came in other lands, other days
unexpected in his mind.
He returned, often, in his dreams
and his flesh, a differing flesh,
returned to that chair, too.

## II  The Dolmen

*About we go, about we go.*
*The procession all, weal and woe,*
*About we go, about we go.*

The earth, the mound to which we go.
The entry dark, the turn within.
Good and sin, good and sin.

They say, "Here is death",
I say "No".
Here we began, weal and woe.
Here lie the begotten,
once begetting,
Spirit lingers unforgetting.

*About we go, about we go.*
*The procession all, weal and woe.*

Here is the end.
I say "No".
Here are the once begotten
Some unforgetting, some unforgotten.

No, no tomb.
This is a womb.

## III  Broken Palings

It looks languorous,
the fence flows with the slope of the sand.
It has an elegance,
a passage of rhythm
terminated.

This slinking beauty,
like a snake,
has a sting.

Two hands cannot straighten it;
it contains a wily strength
that twists with sullen energy.

Defiance has
a loveliness.

## IV  Singapore

The cypripediums stand straight
the cattleyas recline,
others are little tufts
in pots.
Some are tall and waylaying,
blooms nose his shirt.
This balcony was
where he was earthed.
He needed that.
He leant on the rail
and saw the sea aflash
as always in the sun.
No change here.
The island across the straits
rose greenly
ships moved decorously
at anchor.
Below in the wide street
the palms, the cannas.
A large leaf fell
to break the barren fastidiousness.
With a pang he saw
a woman with a broom tidy it away.

He went to mix a drink,
he put down his glass,
drinking was monotonous,
like the lack of seasons.

He had known when he came,
known very well,
but the perpetual haunting
by hedgerow memories
he had not expected.

His first rush from this city
had been inland.
To walk in a wood.

The density amazed,
a suffocation of leaves, dying, dead
rotted underfoot:
the clutching creepers,
the gilled parasites,
horizontal trunks.
Myopia in the jungle,
no distance, no horizon:
a tangled Genesis.

It was always Summer,
always Spring,
always Autumn.
Where was Winter?

He longed for change,
feel frost upon his cheek,
cold rain and snow.
He wanted mutation,
a hiccup in the pattern
of the year.

He smiled.
On the bedroom wall
was Autumn. A cottage
the warmth of summer still,
but with a builder, looking ahead,
strengthening the chimney stack.

In snow the old owner
walks with firm care
to the same cottage,
leaving a grey track
on the white ground.

Summer he looked at least
too much abundance,
too familiar.

Spring he never viewed
without a sigh,
there it was under a new moon,
Easter only a week away.

Lambs with dams stand close,
and the gold of daffodils drained
in the cool light
and nobody out of doors.

He smiled again,
drank his drink
without desperation,

went to the balcony,
watched the evening crowds,
rejoiced in the purple
and orange of his Strelitzia
and said aloud,
"Only six more years".

## V Gated Entry

Unseen, unheard
they screamed panic threats,
"Keep out, Keep out"
Crying with insistent silence,
guarding the void.

Time predictably
rushed and ambled by,
trundling through obeying centuries.
Heed was given
and awe was won.

Another age and observation
with rulers, rods and measures
enquiringly disturbed
the detritus
and guardians disappeared.

The curious picnickers poked
with walking sticks
chattering between gulps of lemonade
and further exiled the unseen existers.

The cave, now pissing place
of beast and man
stinks of mortality.

It had to be secured.
Gates forged and fashioned
grip with pinions
the patient stone.

Awe and imagination
had guarded, once,
better by far.

## VI  Llanberis Lake

All converges to a point
and meets.
The horizontal line of startled white
receives the arrow of downpoured light.
It is a mingled meeting
of known unknown.

A rarity,
spoken of seldom;
it tinges a lifetime.
Undefinable
but very definite.
This ecstasy Kilvert saw
on a March day in 1871.

It is to be shared,
but not with everyone.

## VII  Locked Door

What is locked inside?
It lingers,
moulders without use,
Time, always on the move,
here
stands nearly still.
This is a costly preservation.

There's a shudder in the shoulders
and to underline it all,
Dog's Mercury grows
poisonously. It will mask the lock.
But it is free outside.
There are dangers,
it can work its will.

## VIII  Past, Present and Future

The shadows muster, group
and obscure:
making the known unknown
and unsure the relied-upon realities.
But a hand outstretched
touches the spindles of the
spinning wheel.
Endless thread woven
over ended days,
telling the tread and time
of families dead,
woven into warp and weft of memory.

Darkness has won.
With a decisive move
the chair is left,
the lamp lit.
Memories vanish,
shooed like chickens
into a pen and
the door tightly shut
in the twilight.
The wheel spins
the treadle makes
the beat and impetus
and the wool is pulled.
There is thread again
and the future meanders ahead.

## IX  Secrets

Huge slab steps
led
to a modern house.
The steps are pre-lapsarian.
The woman who washed them,
knew, from the chapel,
about the flood, about the fall,
but missed every time,
the fossilled frond
beneath her hand.

She turns to the too tidy garden,
the unspoken is there
amid the outer as well as
inner walls.
There is a distillation here
that permeates
not unpleasantly.

This is a house with a secret
kept.
Not many of these in Wales:
it is a land of secrets,
but they are open,
or certainly half known.

# COMPLETE COMPREHENSION
*On seeing a bust of Prince Ernst Ludwig of
Hesse in Darmstadt*

It began very properly
the portrait of a prince
in marble.
Not in uniform,
nevertheless head military,
clipped moustache,
jaw line firm: all the old cliches.

But the brow showed
an odd imbalance
almost invisible.

There was more than one man
in this head
and they were not at war.

He had large dreams
wrecked by war.
Born at the wrong time.

Yes, a marble index
which tells me why
he was loved
all along.

Can you ask for more?
We do.
He did.
Poor man.
Poor us.

# COMMITTEE MEETING

Through the window
the tree moves.
Its indifference is enviable.

The meeting meets
but never connects
in its unprogressive formation.
Grey suited we attend.
I watch the tree
and am only partly spared
the inexact vocabulary,
managerial, cybernetic words.
Consensus, ruling factor,
approximate balance:
a pretentious carapace
to cover nothing.
Heard before,
to be heard again,
but differently,
ephemeral words have a fashion span.

Suddenly, "We must have a reserve."
Yes, a reserve
Plenty of it.
The tree is reserved,
I'm reserved
and the reserve
means another world.

# MEMENTO

"How morbid. How can you hang that
upon your wall?"
It was found, dumped tidily,
between the mountains and the sea,
a neat negation of love.

Mary Pugh had never been in a florist's before.
"Why buy flowers?" she asked,
"They're in the garden
and they only fade."
She sought another kind.
She found the tribute she desired
to pay to John.
Porcelain flowers were purchased
with hands that clasped
across the Great Divide.
The leaves of zinc, some tinted green,
others silvered with aluminium.
"Like the rails he painted every year.
He'd like that."

It went beneath a mushroom of glass
corsetted in a wire cage.
Set upon the marble chippings,
on a sabbath when the sun shone.
It meant three Sundays passed,
because of weather,

"It didn't seem right to put it
in the rain right away."

Every time she looked she loved John
and their quiet life danced.
The forget-me-nots,
thick as fry,
white and stiff
haunted in the rain or sun.

Her brother died.
Angharad, his wife, bought a wreath.
"She went to Carmarthen.'
It was bigger,
it was coloured.
"Then she always was for show."
Mary looked again,
it had a bird as well as hands,
a hawk of a dove hovering.
"Duw, Duw, John would have liked that."
Her wreath never shone so bright again.

Cage, dome, wreath were lifted.
Mary joined her John.
Back went the wreath on the cold coverlet
of the glossy marble bed
like,
like a very pretty nightie case.
The flowers protected, but not divorced
from drear Novembers,

steely Springs and burning sun
bleached to the poignancy
of sharp sheep bones.

The cage rusted, the glass cracked
and the wreath was tossed
tidily away.
"So, you see, there it is
a wraith, a wreath
upon my wall.
It was life, it is love."

# QUARANTINE

He was used, always, to the best of everything,
knowledge of anything else obscure.
Education expensive, fortunately it fitted him.
Prep. school at Seaford, happy days,
broken by a singular delight,
diphtheria.
His mother left husband, home, and nursed him,
six weeks of quarantine in a cottage
without siblings and Society.
They learnt to know and love each other:
they were friends for evermore.

Eton, Christ's and Sandhurst.
Not ineffably distinguished, but enough.
He rowed for his college, played cricket,
and, yes, really read. Kipling, of course,
and Conrad, some Meredith,
and I have his Henry James
inscribed *Cawnpore* inside the cover,
and within, little question marks
in places that puzzled him.

South Africa taught him
the true tangle of the world.
His heart was not in the cause.
It was for his men he fought.
They began to fall like flies,
by flies.

His greatest deed, for which he got no medals,
was in digging the best latrines.
His kitchens provided wrong and vapid tack,
but they were immaculate.
He lost fewer than any other corps.

Even after Pretoria, he had a roundness
of face, of flesh, of eye and mouth.
He was correct, convention was deferred to.
He had an eye for detail, especially wrong
in decorations and uniform;
the handling of cutlery;
bread and butter had to be folded.
He pounced on mispronunciation.

It was his Mother, protected by privilege,
who always knew so much more than she said,
who saw that he was tired.
He smoked too many Turkish cigarettes
and he flurried the Times with discontent.
She knew quite well where he had been.
"My dear, you need a wife."
He only smiled, and then laughed.
Before she left the room,
she took his face, his loved, loved face,
between her hands.
The grey grave eyes were smoky
like his breath entangled in
the thick covert of his moustache.

She was a Rector's daughter, she said,
"It is better to marry than to burn."
Oh, she loved her son.

The marriage was in Westminster.
A place in Wales was bought,
partly because employment was needed there.
He managed farms and envisaged timber mills.
He was in love with wife and life
and never, never bored.

War. His talents were not used.
"There's something, I don't know, Radical?'
Considered a little unsound.
He patiently abided discomforts
and disgusts, but growled aloud
when they happened to his men.
"I've had my luxury," he said,
"my rightful turn has come.
But these poor buggers have known
nothing but the hard."
The Mess thought him a bit of a crank.

A "coal-box" as they were called,
fired at random, lobbed as half a jest,
killed him in the trench at Ypres,
making his inspection one morning.
His men missed him, but not for long,
He was always a leader,
and they followed him.

He was mourned.
His mother remembered and remembered,
Mostly quarantine in a cottage
and only then
her very soldierly, yet somehow
unsoldier son.

# SENTINELS

A firm line set diagonally
on the free beach.
It was a frail bastion but,
nonetheless,
a redoubt of disapproval.
It was defence and attack,
a fortification of canvas
and aluminium: chairs.
Occupied by a quadriga
coated, stockinged, a drab uniform of righteousness.
At points of relief, peppermints were passed
silently.
There was no communication,
just vigilance.

The sun rose, a soft breeze
blew in with the dancing waves
and stirred the thrift to throb
above their heads.
They saw none of this.
They saw flesh
bronzed, pink and white
uncovered and unashamed.
They saw no families,
only sons and daughters of Belial,
disporting with prurient impropriety.

At last, a gaberdine mac
was removed;
a cardigan discarded to reveal
a long black sleeve.
The sun rose higher and still no word.
Then a glance went down the line,
to right, to right, to right:
dumb message received.

The commandant of Calvin's troop
rose, from his pocket drew a duster
and wiped the sand from his chair.

That done, his neighbour too,
performed the ritual,
the next and, then, the next.
*Shake off the very dust from your feet*
*for a testimony against them.*

Upright, rigid, coated once again
each in order left.
God had made it too hot for them.

# THE OLD GOLD WATCH

She dug it up
and scampered in crowing.
She had made our fortunes,
she had struck gold.
She knew of overdrafts,
and was, by nature,
a worker.
She would redeem the time.

Time, jealous of such zeal,
redeemed her instead.
leaving us with an old gold watch
and we buried her.
But I would have you know
you will never have the gold that's her,
that's in my heart.

## PLOVER

The fox got you,
found little meat
and left you to dry.

Though hanging,
your head is proud and turned,
your wings fall stiff and straight,
shoulders slightly humped.
A smart silhouette
in death,
a fashionable phoenix
rising from the shaded tail.
Feathers holding hidden fires,
orange, green and gold,
I had never known before.
A crest in
long and languid curves
and a beak open to utter
the cry that never came.

You are elegant,
like my grandmother's friends
who with their youthful world in disarray
arrayed themselves
with feathers, veils and pearls
defying war and Austerity.

They did it in dying life.
The lapwing does it in death,
so still sings
but with a silent throat.

# INK

Strange liquid, undrinkable,
but it can easily intoxicate:
also bore.
It can reveal trifles,
like time-tables, mere markings of time.
It can contain truths and glories
that mark time for ever.
It can calm and assuage;
confine and conquer;
enshrine and deify;
maim as well as mark.
It can lie achingly through
generations of evil teeth.
It can demolish, but it can build.
This potent liquid
sometimes shoots the heart into the skies.

These particular stains
on the boarded floor
move me.
Ink spilled by Kilvert.
These blots could have been words,
wiped from his mind,
as he mopped up the mess.

## ONE PLACE AND ANOTHER

One place.

Here I spent two blind years
groping.
Why am I here?
Chance propinquity
which turned to curiosity.
This place is tangible, audible,
clearly visible in the sun
and the mid-day meal smells good.
But no sense is touched,
no taste upon my tongue,
still less my mind.
This is a nowhere of my mind.

And another.

Beneath a wide swatch of sky
bright with light of a nearby sea,
I stand where I have never been.
A flat field, fading dahlias,
screening trees.
Here is happiness, here is unhappiness,
the inner see-saws of the young.
A place of passion, a concentrate of reality.
This gate which I never climbed
is part of me, when Copperfield.

Here is a past more significant
than episodes of mine
deemed fact.
This is a somewhere in my mind.

## WELSH WATER JUG

It isn't, of course,
It was made in Stourbridge
but went to Llanwrtyd
as a wedding present.

Cherished, cleaned, it always gleamed
so that the fern engraved
trapped a furtive granulated light
solemnly:
it added form, a shadowed delicacy
arching, dipping
an Edwardian aesthetic.

This glass had a place
in a chaste and even-tempered home.
A proclamation of primness,
a position superior
asserted in a peasant world.
It was not gentry, unbelieving and unsaved.
This was a puritan fastness,
Chapel:
A deacon at every meal
and every so often the minister.
Frequently a pious hand poured
"the water of life".
It, like the household, kept its station,

gently insisted, important
but not selfly so
in this small straight street.
It was an affirmation of faith
with handle on hip
and a jutting lip.
A blinkered look betrayed
the ignorance of
the flash and splash of wine.
It had never met coloured competition.

This jug, now orphaned, sits
in a dealer's shop.
It remains a token
of its owner's lives:
a correct but not unkind conviction,
a defined apartness deemed divine.

## LOGICAL DREAM

The face in the glass was mine.
It looked at me and
we approved. What else?
Too late to quarrel at this stage.

I spoke, I listened,
but could not catch my words.
"Why, of course, it is a mirror."
So they are bound to be
the round way wrong.

## THIN TIDE

Duncan Jennings,
In memory of
his life, his death on Piper Alpha
last year.
I sit on his seat.
At my feet
the book carved grave of Anne Bronte.
I eat my sandwiches and wait
for my cousin's funeral.

Sun dazzles,
the sea glitters slowly in,
flat gold patterns.
The divide between
sea and sand is hard to see.
Warm in the sun,
as still as a cat,
my energy is held
alert.
Death is remembered
inscribed upon this seat
and confined and kerbed
at my feet.

The glittering sea is right,
the divide, life death
is hard to see.
It is a thin tide.

## CORNISH CHAPEL WIDOW

We drove by often,
neat graveyard field,
neat white-washed box building.
At the window a half-drawn blind.
The acorn dangled,
possibly tapped the pane,
inside must be partial darkness,
like my own.
If I, a passer-by, should share
my demi-sight,
would we all see,
or would the blind be down completely?

# EPIPHANY AT LLANSTEPHAN

A long mew hung behind me
in the air.
The single buzzard
banked and swerved before me,
imitating the glider
that emulates her.

The weather held its breath.

The church door bade me
close it securely. I did.
It was subdued light
more than darkness inside
and strangely warm.
Gold glowed.
It was the picture,
mediaeval multitudinousness.
Rich, well dressed people crowded
and three kings were present,
one raising his crown politely.
Mary utterly undismayed, even disdainful
sits.
Her lady in waiting makes good
her indifference
and smiles appraising the proffered pots.

Right picture. Right day, Epiphany,
the showing of Jesus
to unknown knowing men.
Blackness: a cloud blocks the colours,
only the gold looms white.
Sun returns but
I remain an unwise man.

I close the door securely,
everything pauses,
even the farmers fencing the field.
We wait, we work;
we have waited a long time.